LOCALS GUIDE FOR NONLOCALS

LA JOLLA
GUIDEBOOK

Derek & Andrea Searancke

www.LocalsGuidePublications.com

Introduction

Explore. Discover. Experience.

Whether you're a visitor, new to the area, or a local who hasn't yet explored La Jolla, this guidebook will direct you to the very best La Jolla has to offer.

*Explore...*18 must-see attractions and hidden gems, including seals at the Children's Pool, views atop Mt. Soledad, best beaches, parks, and art walks.

*Discover...*20 maps detail each attraction location, amenities, local shops, and where to eat.

*Experience...*Some of the best things in life are free, even in La Jolla. Local freebies include beautiful ocean views, spotting local marine life (e.g. dolphins, seals, sea lions), and swimming or snorkeling amongst kelp forests and protected reefs.   You can explore art outdoors or wander galleries in the village. You can even enjoy free music around town. This book guides you to all these activities and more.

La Jolla Guidebook is a labor of love for La Jolla, its beaches, wildlife, and fabulous activities. It was written, enjoyed, and heavily photographed by a happy local couple who have lived here over 10 years. Consider this book as your local guide to help you enjoy, explore, discover, and experience La Jolla.

Help Keep This Guide Up to Date

Every effort has been made to ensure the La Jolla Guidebook is accurate. However, many things change after publication: businesses close or come under new management, trail conditions vary, beach access changes, etc. We would love to hear from you concerning your experiences using this guide and we encourage you to post comments and suggestions at www.facebook.com/LaJollaGuidebook.

www.LaJollaGuidebook.com

How To Use This Book

Top attractions to explore during your visit are organized geographically from south to north as listed on the La Jolla map (pg. 5) and contents pages (pg. 6-7). Each attraction has detailed information and a local map to help you enjoy your stay and navigate the area. Local maps include the following:

Amenities: Icons denote viewpoints, restrooms, showers, swimming, trails, picnic tables, etc. See map key below.

Local Food, Activities, and Shops: Colored circles and numbers correspond to "Restaurants, Activities, Shops, etc." business listings beginning on page 58.

Where to Surf: The surfer icon and corresponding number designates surf breaks detailed on page 57.

Map Key

Icon	Description
	Barbeque
	Restrooms
	Beach
	Coastal Access
	Fire Pit
	Trail
	Trail Route
	Parking
	Picnic Tables
	Showers

Icon	Description
	Snorkeling
	Surf Break
	Swimming
	Tide Pools
	Viewpoint
	Restaurants, Cafes
	Essentials
	Surf, Kayak, Bike, etc.
	Museums and Libraries
	Shops

San Diego County

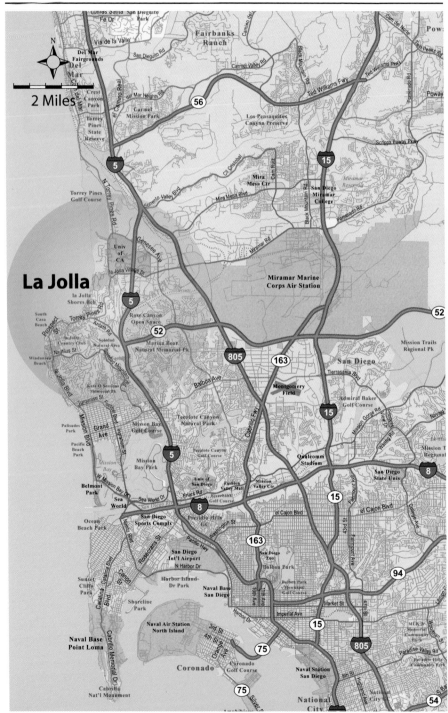

La Jolla Map

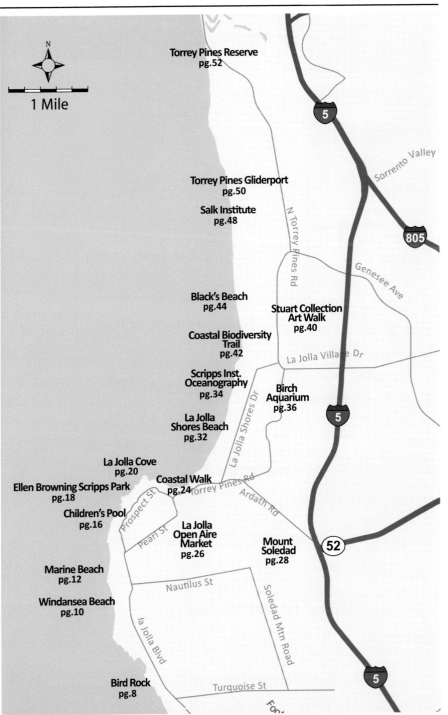

N

1 Mile

Torrey Pines Reserve
pg.52

5

Sorrento Valley

Torrey Pines Gliderport
pg.50

Salk Institute
pg.48

N Torrey Pines Rd

805

Genesee Ave

Black's Beach
pg.44

Stuart Collection
Art Walk
pg.40

Coastal Biodiversity
Trail
pg.42

La Jolla Village Dr

Scripps Inst.
Oceanography
pg.34

Birch
Aquarium
pg.36

La Jolla
Shores Beach
pg.32

La Jolla Shores Dr

5

La Jolla Cove
pg.20

Coastal Walk
pg.24

Torrey Pines Rd

Ardath Rd

Ellen Browning Scripps Park
pg.18

Prospect St

Children's Pool
pg.16

La Jolla
Open Aire
Market
pg.26

Mount
Soledad
pg.28

52

Pearl St

Marine Beach
pg.12

Nautilus St

Windansea Beach
pg.10

Soledad Mtn Road

La Jolla Blvd

Bird Rock
pg.8

Turquoise St

5

Contents

Contents

Bird Rock

Calumet Park

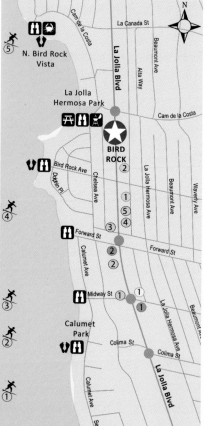

Bird Rock

Bird Rock, a quaint coastal community, attracts visitors and locals alike with a fabulous mix of restaurants, eclectic shops, seaside parks, and stunning vistas. The village gets its name from a prominent rock (albeit eroding) that attracts a slew of sea birds, located at the end of Bird Rock Avenue. The main street, stretching a few blocks, is discernible once you hit a

Downtown Bird Rock

Bird Rock

series of roundabouts and see charming storefronts. Here you can create wearable art at the bead store, experience a coffee "cupping" with the Bird Rock Coffee roaster, or savor California cuisine. You can also browse boutiques or rent a bike at Bird Rock Surf Shop.

The main attractions, however, are the costal parks and vistas featuring picturesque coves, sandstone cliffs and sea grass covered reefs. The rugged shoreline lacks a sandy beach but at very low tides has excellent tide pooling.

Calumet Park is perched on a small coastal bluff with park benches to admire the ocean view and watch surfers. Its grassy lawn is perfect for kids and dogs, and has a mid-morning yoga class held most weekends. Coastal access is via a short path to a rocky beach below.

La Jolla Hermosa Park is a small rocky park with benches, picnic tables, and a BBQ overlooking a lovely cove, but no coastal access. The shoreline is accessible at N. Bird Rock Vista on Camino de la Costa or the end of Bird Rock Avenue.

La Jolla Hermosa Park

N. Bird Rock Coastal Access

Calumet Park

Windansea Beach

Windansea Beach Walkway

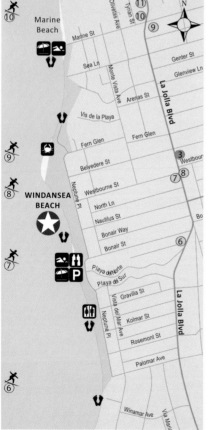

Windansea Beach

Windansea Beach is steeped in surfing history that dates back to the 1940s. It gained national notoriety in 1968, when acclaimed East Coast, counterculture author Tom Wolfe wrote a portrayal of the California beach lifestyle in *The Pump House Gang*. Three well-known surf breaks are scattered along the beach, named respectively from south to north, Big Rock, Wind-

S. Windansea Beach

Windansea Beach

Windansea Low Tide

ansea, and Simmons. These are high performance waves that hold large swells and attract an unforgiving, super-competitive crowd. A handful of park benches provide great vantage points to watch surfers and admire the view.

Windansea's prominent feature is a palm-thatched palapa, a designated historical landmark. It's a popular, picturesque beach, with a few natural sandstone alcoves that provide shelter from crosswinds and privacy from other beachgoers. It's a perfect spot to settle into for the day.

The beach is great for swimming, but be aware the ocean transitions from shallow to deep water quickly, and powerful shore break is possible. If waves look too threatening for a tranquil swim for you or the little ones, La Jolla Cove (pg. 20) or La Jolla Shores (pg. 32) may provide a kinder, gentler option.

Parking: Lot is tiny, but neighboring streets offer a plethora of options.
Amenities: Minimal, come prepared.
Lifeguards present during peak season.

Windansea Sunset

Windansea Palapa

Windansea Beach

Marine Beach

N. Marine Beach

Marine Beach

Marine Beach is easily missed if unfamiliar to the area, less crowded than its neighbors, and one of the best beaches in La Jolla. Because this stretch of coastline is not readily visible to drive-by traffic, you may find more locals than tourists lounging beachside. During winter you may even have it to yourself! It is located a walkable five minutes north of the more populated

N. Marine Beach Tide Pools

Marine Beach

Windansea Beach (pg. 10) via a series of easily negotiated, rocky sandstone outcroppings. It is also accessible by short paths or stairs, leading to either the beach's southern, middle, or northern ends, marked by the "feet" icon on the corresponding map.

When the sea is calm, Marine Beach is great for ocean lovers of all ages and swimming abilities, with good snorkeling at the northern tip. Just be conscious of a steep drop off from shallow to deep water. During larger swells, the beach has a different personality; it turns into a heaving shore break, excellent for experienced body surfers.

To the north, white sand turns to rocky sandstone fingers with many nooks and crannies perfect for tide pooling. You're sure to see anemones, starfish, hermit crabs, and many other critters at low tide.

S. Marine Beach Access

Parking: Street.
Amenities: Minimal, come prepared.
Lifeguards present during summer peak season and holidays.

Marine Beach

Bird Rock, La Jolla Hermosa Park

Children's Pool

Children's Pool

Seaward of Seawall

Children's Pool

Originally intended for children, now inhabited by happy California harbor seals, the La Jolla Children's Pool is a must-see for any visitor.

In 1931, funds donated by revered philanthropist Ellen Browning Scripps resulted in the construction of a crescent shaped seawall, thereby creating a tranquil, open ocean beach pool. The wall effectively shelters the beach from rough seas and yields calm, clear, pool-like waters. It's prime, safe, real estate for sunbathing, napping, and swimming. The area is loved not only by people, but also by seals.

The furry pinnipeds began arriving in the 1990s, and seemed to have staked claim with their perpetual presence. These marine beach bums find the location ideal to rear their young, and from February to April you may see little baby seal pups taking their first few

Children's Pool

Children's Pool

paddles in the ocean. Not all locals are thrilled with the seals. The Children's Pool is the site of a fierce legal battle as to who, human versus seal, should inhabit the aqua waters and fine sand. With the seals constant presence the pool has been deemed by certain governmental agencies too polluted for human frolicking. Some people want the seals ousted, the beach cleaned and returned to the use initially intended, a children's pool.

No matter what side of the debate you lean toward, most visitors and locals alike are thrilled to get an up-close look at seals. Make sure to walk out onto the seawall to get a great view (while keeping an eye out for rogue waves). Don't forget to glance over the seaward side of the wall. When ocean clarity is good you may see California's state fish, the bright orange garibaldi, and other fish swimming amongst the green sea grass.

Parking: Street, if you're lucky.
Amenities: Restrooms, showers, and lifeguards.

Beach Invasion

Walkway S. Of Children's Pool

Seals & Seawall

Children's Pool

Ellen Browning Scripps Park

Boomers Beach

Ellen Browning Scripps Park

Ellen Browning Scripps Park stretches along the Pacific Ocean from La Jolla Children's Pool (pg. 16) to La Jolla Cove (pg. 20). It's one of the most scenic sections of coastline with small cliffs sheltering cozy stretches of golden sand. There is a paved sidewalk that parallels the shore with multiple access points to beautiful beaches below. At the park's north end you will find public restrooms, showers, lifeguards, and a huge expanse of lush green grass that's perfect for picnics and Frisbee.

The quaint, white building within the park is the La Jolla Cove Bridge Club, where you may observe members playing a spirited game of cards. To be "dealt" into the fun, visit the club's website for information. You may also witness a wedding or special event, as the facility is often rented for functions.

Coastal Walkway

Ellen Browning Scripps Park

Ellen Browning Scripps Park

Boomers Beach, just west of the bridge club, is a spectacular body surfing spot, and not for the faint of heart when swells are big. (Sorry, no surf or body boards allowed here.) When the ocean is calm, this beach is great for uncrowded snorkeling and lollygagging. Beware of submerged rocks near the shoreline when sand levels are low.

Park View N.E.

During summer, from approximately July to early September, you can enjoy free, family friendly music courtesy of La Jolla Concerts by the Sea. Sundays, from 2:00 PM to 4:00 PM, settle in on the grassy lawn with your beach chairs, blankets, a picnic of goodies, and enjoy the music. (FYI: no alcohol allowed.) The performance varies weekly and can range widely from big band to rock. Visit ljconcertsbythesea.org for a current schedule.

Picnic In The Park

Parking: Street, if you're lucky, or nearby pay lots.
Amenities: Restrooms, showers, picnic tables, lifeguards, & BBQs.
Web: lajollacovebridgeclub.org, ljconcertsbythesea.org

Ellen Browning Scripps Park

Ellen Browning Scripps Park

La Jolla Cove

La Jolla Cove

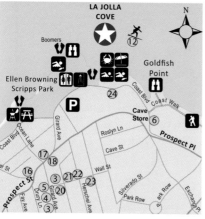

Clam C

La Jolla Cove

La Jolla Cove, or simply the Cove, is a small, beautiful, white sand beach that attracts hundreds of thousands of visitors each year. It's the best spot for open water swimming and snorkeling, with water clarity up to 30 feet!

The Cove is located at the north end of Ellen Browning Scripps Park and is easily accessible via steep stairs. The surrounding sandstone cliffs provide shelter from prevailing winds and waves, thereby making the beach seem warmer and calmer than its neighbors.

Snorkeling and diving here are fantastic, not only because of water clarity, but also because of abundant sea life and kelp forests. The waters off the Cove fall within the boundaries of the 6,000-acre La Jolla Underwater Park, and include an Ecological Reserve. Word of the protected perimeter has obviously spread to marine life, because they

La Jolla Cove

happily flourish here, where fishing and scavenging are not allowed. Even the shells and rocks must stay put! You're sure to see California's state fish, the "melt-down" orange garibaldi. You'll probably see seals, barracuda, opaleye, and bait fish too.

Water Clarity Up To 30 Feet

For open water swimming, the Cove is a favorite. There are distance markers to measure your efforts (¼ mile buoy, ½ mile buoy, and 1 ½ miles to the pier each way). Looking for a swim buddy? Members of the La Jolla Cove Swim Club swim here all year. Ask around or check the club's website to swim with a local. Make sure you have good goggles because you'll want to see what you're swimming with other than humans. You may be lucky enough to see a giant sea bass (500 lb worth), an eagle ray, or even a sea turtle.

Swimmers, Snorkelers, Sunbathers

Parking: Street, if you're lucky, or nearby pay lots.
Amenities: Restrooms, showers, and lifeguards, who diligently protect beach visitors year round.
Web: lajollacoveswimclub.org

The Cove & Ellen Browning Scripps Park

Windansea Beach

Coastal Walk

Sea Caves from Goldfish Point

Sea Lion

Coastal Walk

The Coastal Walk is a short stroll that should be on your to-do list. The 10-minute one-way walk takes you from La Jolla Cove (pg. 20) to what we call the "7 Sea Caves Lookout." Just a warning, the stroll may take longer, as you will want to dawdle along the way.

From the Cove the walk heads northeast along the sidewalk, hugging the coast-

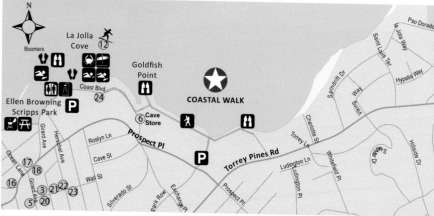

Coastal Walk

line. You'll pass a slew of sea birds on the cliff's edge where it appears birds of a feather indeed flock together. Each species seems to have staked out invisible boundaries for assembling. You're sure to see, as well as smell, clusters of cormorants, sleeping giant Brown Pelicans, and a variety of gulls huddled in packs. You may also see seals and sea lions. Spot the differences: Sea lions have external ear flaps and hairless flippers which they use to "walk"; seals, however, have ear holes and can only wiggle their way on land. During summer, the ocean can get a bit congested (like going to a state fair opening day). Watching the uncoordinated chaos of people swimming, snorkeling, and kayaking, while mixing with marine life, can be very entertaining.

Kayaks at Goldfish Point

For the landlubber who wants to explore a sea cave, but doesn't want to get wet doing it, you could make a detour to the Cave Store. Within the eclectic shop, you'll find a manmade tunnel dug entirely by pick and shovel (completed in 1903). For a few dollars you can descend the 145 steps and witness the geological wonder of Sunny Jim Cave, no wetsuit necessary. Before you reach the Cave Store the Coastal Walk veers left and follows a dirt footpath, near a viewing platform at Goldfish Point. The path continues east, above the cliffs, over a little bridge and around to a point where you can see the marvelous seven sea caves.

Goldfish Point

FYI: For a longer walk, start at the Children's Pool (pg. 16).
Parking: Street or nearby pay lots.
Cave Store: 1325 Coast Blvd.

Coastal Walk View N

Coastal Walk

La Jolla Open Aire Market

Fresh Fruit, Veg. And Flowers

La Jolla Open Aire Market

La Jolla Open Aire Market, where farm fresh produce mingles with local artisan crafts, chichi knick-knacks, and yummy food stalls that make you wish your stomach was twice the size to taste everything.

Every Sunday, rain or shine, locals and visitors gather at the market to restock their pantry, visit with farmers, vendors and friends, and of course, indulge in the all-too tempting samples of fantastic food on offer.

Local farmers provide a great selection of organic veggies, fragrant herbs, and handpicked fruit. In addition to produce, you may also find spicy salsa, garlicky hummus, or fresh baked bread. If you're looking for a quick bite, head over to the food stalls and sink your teeth into "street" tacos, savory crepes,

Vendor Stalls

La Jolla Open Aire Market

or a mouthwateringly tender BBQ beef sandwich. Craving something sweet? You may find homemade fudge, churros stuffed with custard, kettle corn, or oddly-good rosemary cookies.

Need a gift? Peruse the offerings created by local artists such as handmade jewelry, distinctive note cards, driftwood sculptures, or original oil paintings. You can also find fresh cut flowers, great sun hats, or local photos.

Need something for the home? You may find the perfect Persian rug, a fine selection of table linens, beautiful baskets, or even plants for the garden.

Venders may vary, so no two visits are the same, but one thing is certain: You're bound to find something you can't (or don't really want to) live without.

Parking: Street, if you're lucky, and nearby lots.
Amenities: Restrooms, picnic tables.
Where: 7335 Girard Avenue.
When: Sundays, 9:00 AM - 1:00 PM.

Mediterranean Treats

Morning Snack

Picnic At The Market

La Jolla Open Aire Market

Mount Soledad

View S.W. Of Mission Bay

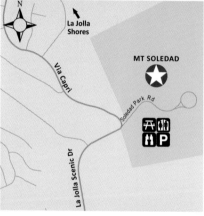

Mt. Soledad Cross

Mount Soledad

Looming 822 feet above sea level, Mt. Soledad Natural Park provides awe-inspiring, 360-degree panoramic views of the entire county and beyond. It's a great place to find your bearings and see spectacular scenery. Looking north you'll notice La Jolla Shores coastline, towering Torrey Pines cliffs, and on a clear day, the San Bernardino Mountains. Westward is the mighty Pacific Ocean and La Jolla Village. To the south, you can see from Mission Bay and the San Diego skyline, all the way to the hills of Tijuana, Mexico.

Fittingly, Mt. Soledad Veterans Memorial is perched atop this picturesque hill, and provides a perfect setting to pay tribute to veterans who served our country, preserving the freedoms we enjoy. The memorial is unique as it honors veterans from every branch of the US military, spanning the Revolutionary War to present day conflicts. Most plaques

Mount Soledad

contain an image of the veteran and a brief summary of service, making it a very personal experience. There are even plaques that jointly honor husband and wife veterans, platoons, and former presidents.

Amenities are minimal, with the primary objective to enjoy the view and honor those who have given the ultimate sacrifice. A few park benches and a grassy lawn provide great spots to relax and admire the setting.

The memorial's current centerpiece is a hotly contested, towering cross constructed and dedicated to veterans in 1954. The presence of the cross on public land arguably violates separation of church and state, with some requesting its removal. The city subsequently sold parkland to the private Memorial Association. Unfortunately, the legitimacy of this sale is also contested, and the controversy continues.

Parking: Free lot, small but ample.
Amenities: Benches.
Where: 6905 La Jolla Scenic Drive S.
When: Hours 7:00 AM - 10:00 PM.

View S. Of San Diego Skyline

Memorial Plaques

View N. Of Torrey Pines Cliffs

Mount Soledad

Coastal Walk, Goldfish Point

La Jolla Shores Beach

© La Jolla Shores Beach

La Jolla Shores

La Jolla Shores is a lovely mile-long stretch of wide, sandy beach that has something for everyone. The southern end is perfect for water lovers of all ages and abilities, with its frequently calm conditions and smaller, gentler waves, compared to the middle and northern shores. It's kid friendly, not only because of the shallow sand shelf that gradually drops to deeper waters, but also because there's a fun playground adjacent to the boardwalk at Kellogg Park. The grassy lawns at Kellogg Park are perfect for picnics, BBQs, volleyball, or assembling diving equipment without sand clinging to all your gear and goodies.

As for activities, La Jolla Shores is great for diving since the underwater La Jolla Canyon, with ledges dipping to depths of 50 to 800+ feet, is in close proximity. With only a snorkel and mask you can see some amazing marine life too.

La Jolla Shores Beach

Harmless leopard sharks (yes, truly harmless) congregate just off shore of the Marine Room Restaurant to breed annually. Peak viewing is early summer. Sometimes you don't even need a mask for viewing, just wade out to hip deep water and keep your eyes peeled for up to seven foot dark moving shapes. You're sure to see stingrays too, as they frequent the area. It's advisable to do the "stingray shuffle" (shuffle your feet as you wade instead of taking airborne steps) to prevent startling rays into stinging mode.

Kellogg Park

For kayaking to La Jolla Cove (pg. 20), head to the boat launch at the end of Avenida de la Playa to begin your adventure. No kayak? No worries. You can rent one along the same street in the village of La Jolla Shores. You can also enroll in surf school, rent snorkeling gear, or purchase anything else you may need in this little town too.

Parking: Free Kellogg Park lot, street.
Amenities: Restrooms, showers, lifeguards, playground, a few shade trees, picnic tables, BBQs, and fire pits.

Beach Boardwalk

La Jolla Shores

La Jolla Shores Beach

Scripps Inst. Oceanography

Scripps Pier & La Jolla Village

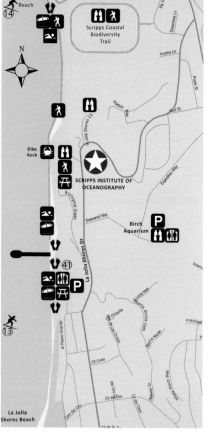

Scripps Institute of Oceanography

Scripps Institute of Oceanography (SIO or Scripps for short) is a world-renowned research facility and University of California San Diego (UCSD) graduate school specializing in atmosphere, oceanography, and earth sciences. Its idyllic location encompasses the north end of La Jolla Shores Beach (pg. 32), the 1,084-foot pier, and neighboring hillsides. It also includes Birch Aquarium (pg. 36), where SIO's research discoveries are shared through interactive programs and exhibits. Wander the grounds to discover numerous vantage points and meandering walkways that offer scenic ocean views.

Although the pier is usually closed to the general public, you can still finagle your way on by participating in a full moon pier walk. From June to October you can arrange a tour, via Birch Aquarium,

Scripps Inst. Oceanography

to join a naturalist for a moonlit stroll on the pier. The evening activities may include dissecting squid, making plankton glow, and observations of other nocturnal marine creatures. For more moonlit fun, you can also witness a grunion run. Grunion is a tiny fish that comes to shore to spawn in the sand during (and 3 days after) full and new moon lit nights. For more information, visit dfg.ca.gov/marine/grunionschedule.asp.

There's great tide pooling at Dike Rock a few hundred yards north of the pier within Scripps Coastal Reserve. You can walk along the coast to Black's Beach (pg. 44) or Torrey Pines Beach & Reserve (pg. 52) from here too.

Hungry and don't want to fish for a meal? Try Caroline's Seaside Café by the pier. It serves breakfast and lunch with seasonal organic offerings, reasonable prices, and great ocean views.

Parking: Street, UCSD lot, or La Jolla Shores/Kellogg Park lot (pg. 32).
Amenities: Picnic tables, lifeguards.

Under The Pier

Caroline's Seaside Cafe

Sunset

Scripps Inst. Oceanography

Birch Aquarium

Kelp Forest

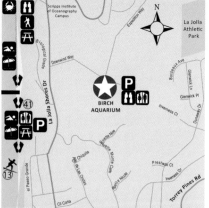

Birch Aquarium

Want to discover what's beneath the ocean surface without getting wet? Visit Birch Aquarium. The aquarium, part of University of California San Diego (UCSD) Scripps Institute of Oceanography (pg. 34), provides a forum where the latest discoveries and research are communicated to the masses through dioramas and interactive displays.

A favorite exhibit is the Hall of Fishes, which provides detailed information of local Pacific Ocean fishes, sea floor geography, currents, and winds. You can observe what lies beneath the ocean surface along the La Jolla coast, including the La Jolla and Scripps submarine canyons. The exhibits demonstrate why an abundance of marine life flocks to the area and provides living examples of local species. The 70,000-gallon kelp forest tank provides a very realistic view of what you may witness when diving

Tropical Fish

Birch Aquarium

off La Jolla Cove (pg. 20). It's a great way to help identify which local marine life may be within arm's reach during your next swim.

For hands-on discovery, head to the outdoor plaza with three interactive tide pools and views of the La Jolla coast. You can touch, feel, and see a host of local marine critters. Docents are available to answer any questions. If you want to see more fish in action, make sure to check the aquarium's daily feeding schedules.

Gray Whale Sculpture

Birch Aquarium also organizes fun outdoor adventures, such as full moon pier walks and grunion runs. In addition, you can watch the sunset at the tide pool plaza while listening to great music at one of the summertime Green Flash Concerts. Check the website for a schedule of events and performances.

Parking: First 3 hours free.
Amenities: Cafe, bookstore, restrooms.
Where: 2300 Expedition Way.
When: Daily: 9:00 AM - 5:00 PM.
Web: birchaquarium.org

Tide Pool

Tide Pool Plaza

Birch Aquarium

Stuart Collection Art Walk

Fallen Star

Stuart Collection Art Walk

Discover a treasure trove of outdoor art at the University of California San Diego (UCSD). Intermingled amongst the lecture halls and libraries of this 1,200-acre campus are, at current count, 18 varied artworks created by some of the leading artists of our time. Collectively known as the Stuart Collection, these art pieces are best viewed on foot, via a 2.5 hour walking tour at USCD campus. Not only will you get your exercise and a dose of culture, but also experience the UCSD campus without the worries of lugging textbooks or cramming for exams.

The Stuart Collection brochure and art tour map is available (and a necessity to enjoy the tour) at UCSD's Visitor Info Center, online, via request by mail, or as a self-titled downloadable app. It provides artwork location and detailed

Stuart Collection Art Walk

information of each artist and associated works featured along the walk.

You can see a gargantuan, 180 ton, 23-foot-6-inch tall bear made of granite boulders, walk along a giant serpent's scales through a mini Garden of Eden, witness trees emitting music, poems, and chants, and pay tribute to a colorful bird-like *Sun God*. The newest installation, called *Fallen Star*, looks akin to a scene from *The Wizard of Oz*, with Dorothy's quaint house precariously perched seven stories high, on Jacobs Hall. It is surrounded by a lovely rooftop garden, and acts as a home away from home for its visitors.

If you want to learn more about the artworks, short videos are available for viewing at UCSD's Geisel Library in the film and video section.

Parking: Free on weekends, permits required weekday via info kiosks, meters.
Web: stuartcollection.ucsd.edu
Info Center: Gilman Drive, near UCSD Gilman entrance. Staffed 10-7, weekdays, 10-5 weekends, closed holidays.

Sun God

Trees & Geisel Library

Bear

Stuart Collection Art Walk

Coastal Biodiversity Trail

Trail View S.

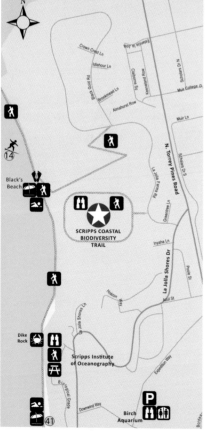

Coastal Biodiversity Trail

High above the Pacific Ocean, perched atop rugged cliffs, is the Scripps Coastal Reserve Biodiversity Trail. The trail occupies approximately 15% of the reserve's nearly 1,000 acres and provides jaw-dropping views of La Jolla and surrounding coastline. The reserve encompasses a wide range of terrain both above and below the ocean, including cliffs, canyons, tide pools, beach, and a scenic biodiversity trail meandering through grassy, coastal sage scrubland.

This area, often referred to as the Knoll, is 350 feet above the ocean, bordered by Black's Canyon to the north, and Sumner Canyon to the south. Don't worry, you won't have to scale cliffs or climb canyons to reach the trail. The entrance is easily accessible 0.1 mile along La Jolla Farms Road, on the left.

Coastal Biodiversity Trail

The Biodiversity Trail is a mainly flat, half-mile interpretive loop through Mediterranean-type landscape, once typical of San Diego County. Its former occupants include the La Jolla Indians (8,000 years ago), grazing cattle, Texan oil tycoon-turned-farmer named Black, and soldiers who trained and used the area as a lookout during World War II.

Coastal Biodiversity Trail

Although small, the reserve's diversity is big, with over 200 plant species, 88 bird species, and 12 mammal species. Bring a field guide and see how many you can identify. If you're lucky, trail guides will be stocked near the entrance, underneath the large trail sign, which provide detailed information about what you'll see in the reserve. Don't worry if there aren't any available, as interpretive plaques provide similar information along the trail.

View Point

FYI: Access Black's Beach (pg. 44) via pedestrian only Black's Road, a further 0.25 mile along La Jolla Farms Road.
Parking: Street.
Amenities: Minimal, come prepared.
Trail: Suitable for all ages.

Trail View N.

Coastal Biodiversity Trail

Black's Beach

Black's Beach

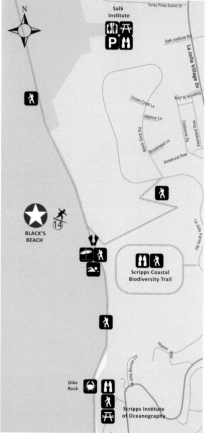

Black's Beach

Black's is famous for scenic beauty, surf, and nudists. It's a gorgeous, golden 2-mile stretch of coast, backed by towering 300-foot cliffs and canyons. The area's rugged beauty has endured partly because access, although not difficult, does require a bit of effort. The shortest routes descend from cliff top via either the unmaintained (yet doable) Gliderport trail (pg. 50), or the

The "Mushroom"

Black's Beach

paved (pedestrian only) Black's Road. Both are an easy decent, but the steep uphill return can elicit some serious huffing and puffing. You may also reach Black's by walking along the coast 1 or 2 miles, respectively, from La Jolla Shores (pg. 32) or Torrey Pines State Beach (pg. 52) at lower tides.

Walking To Black's

Nearby Scripps submarine canyon not only supports a wide array of life, such as dolphins, seals, and migrating whales, but also funnels swells from deep to shallow shores, thereby creating powerful, fast, hollow waves, making this a world-class beach break for experienced surfers. As for nudity, officially it's not permitted, but often is condoned north of the Gliderport trail. It's mainly overexposed middle age men. Prepare to avert your eyes.

Bonus: 1968 architectural gem, aka the "Mushroom," at Black's south end. Designed by Dale Naegle, it serves as a guesthouse for a cliff top home, accessed by private tram & drawbridge.

Amenities: Lifeguards & nothing else.

Black's Road

Black's Beach

Black's Beach

Black's Beach

Salk Institute

Salk Courtyard

Salk Walkway

Salk Institute

Get in touch with your scientific side and explore the Salk: a scientific powerhouse, leading collaboration and innovation in the big business of biotech.

Its creator, Dr. Jonas Salk (developer of the polio vaccine), envisioned an independent research facility where scientists share novel ideas and discoveries, thereby advancing biological studies. With the help of renowned architect Louis Kahn, and San Diego's generous 27 acre gift of prime coastal real estate, a grand structure was born, attracting great minds from around the world (e.g. F. Crick, R. Dulbecco, and many others).

Completed in 1965, the institute was designed from simple materials (concrete, teak, and travertine) that could stand the test of time with minimal maintenance. To promote collaboration among scientists, the structures are

Salk Institute

open plan, labs are easily reconfigured, and there is a central grand courtyard with a few slate walls where graffiti is encouraged to illustrate ideas during impromptu discussions.

Want to do more than look at scientists? Attend a seminar; check the website for schedules and topics.

Concrete, Teak & Travertine

Not interested in science? The Salk is still worthy of a visit to view the architecture. Set on a coastal bluff, overlooking the Pacific Ocean, 2 mirror image structures surround a courtyard where a central water feature aligns with the sun at sunset during spring equinox. Any time of year is a great opportunity to witness the starkly simplistic view. Architectural tours are offered M-F, 12 to 1 PM. Call or register online.

Need some fuel for your brain? Grab some grub at the cafe, find a seat in the courtyard, and enjoy the view.

Reflected Light

Parking: Visitor lot, Gliderport (pg. 50).
Where: 10010 N. Torrey Pines Road.
Web: salk.edu   Ph: 858.453.4100

Mirrored Structures

Torrey Pines Gliderport

Runway & Viewing Area

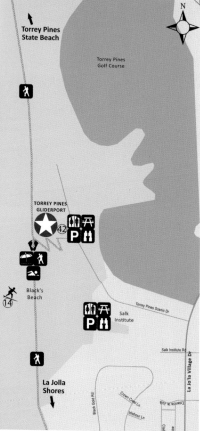

Gliderport

Torrey Pines Gliderport is the perfect place to take a giant (yet calculated) leap of faith and gently step off a cliff. However, to successfully soar like a bird, you'll need a paraglider or hang glider to perfect this feat. Fortunately, the Gliderport offers tandem flights with experienced pilots year round, giving the adventurous the best view in town of the coast, canyons, Torrey

Ready, Steady, Jump

Torrey Pines Gliderport

Pines Reserve and Golf Course. Peak flying conditions are ~12 to 3 PM. Be forewarned, you may become addicted to flying. Luckily, the Gliderport offers novice to advanced paragliding lessons taught by award winning instructors.

Even if you prefer to remain firmly grounded, the Gliderport shouldn't be missed. It's an amazing spectacle to see hang gliders, paragliders, and remote control sailplanes fly so gracefully close overhead, practicing lift-off, landing, and acrobatic maneuvers. Also, the setting couldn't be more idyllic, perched on a cliff overlooking Black's Beach (pg. 44) and the Pacific Ocean. Viewing areas have benches to watch the coordinated chaos of multicolored fabric wings hovering above. There's also a great café with shaded outdoor seating and award winning "best sandwiches with a view."

FYI: Reach Black's Beach via cliff trail.
Parking: Free and plentiful.
Where: 2800 Torrey Pines Scenic Dr.
Fly: Daily, conditions permitting.
Ph: 858.452.9858

Cliffhanger Cafe

Gliderport View S.

Paraglider Over Black's Beach

Torrey Pines Gliderport

Torrey Pines Reserve

Trails To Beach & Flat Rock

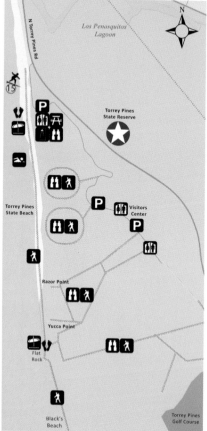

Torrey Pines

Need respite from the concrete jungle? Visit Torrey Pines State Natural Reserve to get your flora & fauna fix. It's certain to satisfy any tree-hugging nature lover with roughly 1,000 acres of rolling hills, sandstone cliffs, coastline, and marshland.

The reserve is named in honor of the rare and stoic Torrey pine found only 2

Beach Trail

Torrey Pines Reserve

places on earth: here, along a 4-mile stretch of spectacular coast including the reserve and an island off the coast of Santa Barbara, called Santa Rosa. You'll enjoy the area even if you aren't an avid arborist. Not only will you witness Torrey's majestic boughs and sturdy trunks clinging to 300-foot coastal cliffs, but you will also see native shrubs, birds, and other critters.

Spring Flowers

The best way to explore the area (and wrap your loving arms around a Torrey pine) is to take a hike. There are numerous short trails, which can be linked together for a longer loop. The views from Yucca and Razor Point are superb, and offer the best vantage to spot dolphins and other marine life.

Trails lead to either the visitor center or beach, both worth exploring. The quaint adobe brick visitor center, built in 1922, has informative exhibits, trail maps, and a film about life in the park.

Torrey Pines Beach

Parking: Multiple lots. Day use fee or pass required. Nearby street parking. Amenities: Restroom, shower, benches.

Razor Point Trail View

Torrey Pines Gliderport

Surf Breaks

Windansea

Black's Beach

Big Rock

Surf Breaks

La Jolla has always been synonymous with surfing and for good reason.

In a relatively short stretch of coastline there is an amazing variety of beaches and reefs that can accommodate swell from various angles, all capable of providing world-class surf when conditions cooperate.

In the winter months, the same huge swells that hammer Alaska and the Hawaiian Islands march onwards, unloading onto the La Jolla coast. During summer, swell is generated by South Pacific storms which sends up well organized, finely manicured lines that break with machine-like precision. Combine these factors with a near perfect climate, relatively warm water, a readily accessible shore, and you're left with one of the most crowded and competitive stretches of coastline you are likely to surf. No swell goes unridden

Surf Breaks

and the atmosphere in the water varies by break, but as a rule don't always expect to be welcomed into the lineup!

You need to be realistic about your abilities before you paddle out, and the old adage rings true: "If in doubt, don't go out." Lifeguards are accessible at many locations, have a wealth of water knowledge, and are there to protect, answer questions, and provide expert advice; so use them.

If you have never surfed, you're in luck! San Diego, specifically La Jolla Shores (pg. 32), has become somewhat of a surf school mecca, with various companies offering expert instruction and equipment rental. Contact details for surf schools and surf shops can be found on page 60.

This surf break list is a rough guide for those exploring the coastline looking for a session. It covers the more well-known breaks and is by no means exhaustive, but will point you in the right direction.

	PAGE #	BREAK NAME	BREAK TYPE	POWER RATING (1 - 3)*
1	8	Hermos	Reef	1
2	8	Hanniman's	Reef	1
3	8	Sewer Line	Reef	1
4	8	South Bird	Reef	2
5	8	North Bird	Reef	2
6	10	Big Rock	Reef	3
7	10	Windansea	Reef	2
8	10	Simmons	Reef	3
9	10	Little Point	Reef	2
10	12	Horsehoes	Reef	3
11	12	Hospitals	Reef	2
12	20	The Cove	Point	3
13	32	La Jolla Shores	Beach	2
14	44	Black's	Beach	3
15	52	Torrey Pines	Beach	2

* **Power Rating** : 1 Forgiving, 2 Grunty, 3 Consequence

Restaurants & Activities

 RESTAURANTS, CAFES, ETC.

1 - Bahia Don Bravo $
Mexican
5504 La Jolla Blvd. | 858.454.8940
Favs: Shrimp burrito, whole fried snapper.

2 - Lupi Vino Cucina Bar $$
Italian Trattoria
5518 La Jolla Blvd. | 858.454.6421

3 - Starbucks $
5604 La Jolla Blvd. | 858.454.4037
905 Pearl Street | 858.454.2801
2206 Torrey Pines Road | 858.454.4423

4 - Julian Bakery $
5621 La Jolla Blvd. | 858.454.1198
Favs: Pies & heavenly breads.

5 - Bird Rock Coffee Roasters $
5627 La Jolla Blvd. | 858.551.1707
Favs: Coffee tasting (cupping) Fridays,10:30 AM.

6 - WindanSea Cafe $
Sandwiches & More
6780 La Jolla Blvd. | 858.459.1895
Favs: Veg-out & Chickanini panini.

7 - Promiscuous Fork $-$$
A Fun Foodie Joint For Lunch & Dinner
6984 La Jolla Blvd. | 858.459.3663
Web: thepromiscuousfork.com

8 - The Shack Bar and Grill $
American
6941 La Jolla Blvd. | 858.454.5280

9 - Rigoberto's $
Mexican
7345 La Jolla Blvd. | 858.551.1817
Favs: Adobada taco, carne asada torta.

10 - Verdes El Ranchero $-$$
Mexican
7404 La Jolla Blvd. | 858.459.5877

11 - Carino's Italian Restaurant $$
7408 La Jolla Blvd. | 858.459.1400
Favs: Sausage, pepperoni, mushroom
pizza (with bait), clam linguine.

12 - Baskin Robbins $
Ice Cream & Frozen Yogurt
7470 La Jolla Blvd. | 858.459.5353

13 - Yogi Topi $
Frozen Yogurt
7501 La Jolla Blvd. | 858.456.1334

14 - Pizza on Pearl $-$$
617 Pearl Street | 858.729.0717
Fav: BCR Pizza (bacon, chicken, caramelized
onion & ranch). Buy a slice or whole pie.

15 - El Pescador Fish Market $-$$
Café and Seafood Market
627 Pearl Street | 858.456.2526
Fav: Local sea bass sandwich.

16 - Nine-Ten Restaurant & Bar $$-$$$
Seasonal California Cuisine
910 Prospect Street | 858.964.5400

17 - Living Room Café & Bistro $
Coffeehouse & more. Open late.
1010 Prospect Street | 858.459.1187

18 - Gelateria Frizzante $
1025 Prospect Street, #130 | 858.454.5798
Favs: Hazelnut gelato.

19 - Brick & Bell $
Breakfast & Lunch
928 Silverado Street | 858.344.5928
Favs: Scones & coconut macaroons.

20 - Girard Gourmet $-$$
Café, Deli, & Bakery
7837 Girard Avenue | 858.454.3325

21 - Whisknladle $$
Seasonal California Cuisine
1044 Wall Street | 858.551.7575
Favs: Tapas & happy hour.

22 - Karl Strauss Brewing Company $$
Craft Beers & Good Pub Grub
1044 Wall Street | 858.551.2739

23 - Coffee Cup $-$$
Breakfast & Lunch
1109 Wall Street | 858.551.8514
Favs: Breakfast sweet corn tamales.

Restaurants & Activities

24 - Goldfish Point Café $
Breakfast & Lunch
1255 Coast Blvd. | 858.459.7407

25 - Museum Cafe $
700 Prospect St | 858-456-6427
Web: giuseppecatering.com

26 - Wahoo's Fish Taco $
Mexican-Hawaiian with a twist
639 Pearl Street | 858.459.0027

27 - Bibby's Crepe Café $
723 Pearl Street | 858.459.0558
Favs: Brit & Mikado crepes.

28 - La Jolla Brew House $-$$
Craft Beers & Pub Grub
7536 Fay Avenue | 858.456.6279

29 - Bernini's Bistro $$
European Bistro
7550 Fay Avenue | 858.4545013

30 - PrepKitchen $$
Seasonal California Cuisine
7556 Fay Avenue, #A | 858.875.7737

31 - Michele Coulon Dessertier $$
Lunch & Desserts
7556 Fay Avenue, #D | 858.456.5098

32 - The Cottage $-$$
Breakfast & Lunch. Dinner in summer.
7702 Fay Avenue | 858.454.8409

33 - Pannikin Coffee & Tea $
7467 Girard Avenue | 858.454.5453

34 - Harry's Coffee Shop $-$$
Breakfast & Lunch
7545 Girard Avenue | 858.454.7381

35 - Come On In! $$
American Bistro
1030 Torrey Pines Road #B| 858.551.1063
Favs: Lamb shanks on Thursdays.

36 - Rimel's Rotisserie $$
American
1030 Torrey Pines Road #E | 858.454.6045

37 - Jeff's Burgers $
2152 Avenida De La Playa | 858.454.8038
Favs: Cheeseburger, gyro, chocolate shake.

38 - The Cheese Shop $
Sandwiches & Deli
2165 Avenida de la Playa | 858.459.3921
Favs: Egg salad, eclectic candy and cheese.

39 - Piatti Ristorante & Bar $$
Italian Trattoria
2182 Avenida De La Playa | 858.454.1589

40 - Squires Café & Deli $
Breakfast & Lunch
8080 La Jolla Shores Drive | 858.456.7576

41 - Caroline's Seaside Cafe $
Breakfast & Lunch
8610 Kennel Way | 858.202.0569
Favs: Chopped salad & Seaside Cafe burger.
Web: giuseppecatering.com

42 - Cliffhanger Café (Gliderport) $
2800 Torrey Pines Scenic Dr. | 858.452.9858
Favs: East-West Wind Turkey sandwich.

 ESSENTIALS

1 - CVS Pharmacy
5495 La Jolla Blvd | 858.456.4830
7525 Eads Avenue | 858.551.0699

2 - La Shore Market & Deli
5590 La Jolla Blvd. | 858.459.7655

3 - 7-Eleven
6953 La Jolla Blvd. | 858.454.3432

4 - Sahel Bazar Market & Deli $
7467 Cuvier Street, Suite C | 858.456.9959
Favs: We love this market! Best fresh fruit,
sandwich wraps & Greek salad.

5 - Vons
Supermarket & Pharmacy
7544 Girard Avenue | 858.454.2620

6 - ATM Bankers Block: Girard Avenue between
Kline & Silverado Streets you'll find Bank of
America, Wells Fargo, and US Bank.

Activities & Shops

 SURF, KAYAK, BIKE, ETC

1 - Bird Rock Surf Shop
Surf Gear, Ding Repair, Board & Bike Rentals
5509 La Jolla Blvd. | 858.459.9200

2 - Mitch's Surf Shop
Surf Gear, Rentals & Clothing
631 Pearl Street | 858.459.5933

3 - We Love Tourists
Segway Tours
7430 ½ Girard Avenue | 619.512.3491
Web: welovetourists.com

4 - La Jolla Surf Systems
Surf Gear, Rentals, Lessons & Clothing
2132 Avenida de la Playa | 858.456.2777

5 - Bike and Kayak Tours, Inc.
Surf, Snorkel, Kayak, Bike Rentals & Tours
2158 Avenida De La Playa | 858.454.1010
Web: bikeandkayaktours.com

6 - Surf Diva Surf School
Surf Gear, Rentals, Lessons & Clothing
2160 Avenida De La Playa | 858.454.8273
Web: surfdiva.com

7 - La Jolla Sea Cave Kayaks
Kayak Rentals & Tours April - October
2164 Avenida de la Playa | 858.454.0111
Web: lajollaseacavekayaks.com

8 - OEX Dive and Kayak
Diving, Paddle Board, Surf, Snorkel, Kayak Tours
and Rental
2243 Avenida De La Playa | 858.454.6195

9 - Hike Bike Kayak
Hike, Snorkel, Kayak, Bike Rentals & Tours
2216 Avenida de la Playa | 858.551.9510
Web: hikbikekayak.com

9 - Menehune Surf
Surf School (Same Address as Hike Bike Kayak)
2216 Avenida de la Playa | 858.663.7299
Web: menehunesurf.com

 MUSEUMS & LIBRARIES

1 - Museum of Contemporary Art San Diego
700 Prospect Street | 858.454.3541
Free 3rd Thursday of month, 5:00 PM – 7:00 PM.

2 - La Jolla Historical Society
7846 Eads Avenue | 858.459.5335
Exhibits and Information.
Web: lajollahistory.org

3 - Athenaeum Music & Arts Library
1008 Wall St. | 858.454.5872
Free Mini-Concerts-at-Noon, some Mondays.
Web: ljathenaeum.org

4 - La Jolla Public Library
7555 Draper Avenue | 858.552.1657
Web: lajollalibrary.org

 SHOPS

1 - Beads Of La Jolla
5645 La Jolla Blvd | 858.459.6134

2 - Gwen Couture
Specialty fabric & notions
5745 La Jolla Blvd | 858.454.8599

3 - Warwick's
Books, gifts & more
7812 Girard Avenue | 858.454.0347

4 - Burns Drugs
Pharmacy, eclectic mix of gifts, etc.
7824 Girard Avenue | 858.459.4285

5 - Bowers Jewelers
Jewelry, gifts, & more behind the counter
7860 Girard Avenue | 858.459.3678

6 - Cave Store
Eclectic mix of jewelry, clothes, curios & cave
1325 Coast Blvd | 858.459.0746

7 - D.G. Wills Books
New & used books
7461 Girard Avenue | 858.456.1800

Extras

TORREY PINES GOLF COURSE

Home of the 2008 US Open and 36 fabulous holes of golf. Public course. Call for tee times.
11480 N. Torrey Pines Road | 877.581.7171
Web: torreypinesgolfcourse.com
Annual PGA Tournament (Farmers Ins. Open)
When: January, ~fourth week.

THE LODGE AT TORREY PINES

The Grill (at Torrey Pines putting green) $$
11480 N. Torrey Pines Road | 858.453.4420
Favs: Grilled Salmon salad, drugstore burger

The Spa at Torrey Pines
11480 N. Torrey Pines Road | 858.453.4420
A beautiful spot to be spoiled, and the decor pays homage to Charles Rennie Mackintosh.
Web: lodgetorreypines.com

ART & MUSIC

First Friday Art Walk
Enjoy a free wander through art galleries in La Jolla Village. Revel in art, music, refreshments, and local restaurant "happy hour" specials.
When: Monthly, first Friday, 6:00 PM – 9:00 PM.

Art in the Pines
An outdoor spring art festival at Torrey Pines State Natural Reserve (pg. 52) with local artists.
When: A weekend event sometime in May.
Web: torreypines.org

CAR AFICIONADOS

La Jolla Concours d'Elegance
An annual classic car show.
When: ~April | Web: lajollaconcours.com

Symbolic Motor Car Company
Drool over Bentley, Bugatti, Lamborghini, Rolls-Royce Motor Cars & classic race cars.
Where: 7440 La Jolla Boulevard

Need a Ferrari or Maserati?
Find one on the corner of Girard & Pearl.
Where: 7514 and 7477 Girard St., respectively.

TRAILS & WALKS

Coastal Walk (pg. 24)
20 min. - 1 hr. Easy. Coastal views.
Stuart Collection Art Walk (pg. 40)
2.5 hr. Easy. Fabulous outdoor art.
Coastal Biodiversity Trail (pg. 42)
30 min. Easy. Coastal views and native flora.
Black's Beach (pg. 44)
15 min. - 1 hr. Easy - moderate, depending on route. Coastal and canyon views, beach.
Torrey Pines Reserve (pg. 52)
15 min. - 2 hr. Easy - moderate, based on route. Coastal and canyon views, native flora, and beach. Numerous trails.

PARADES

Best hometown 4th of July Parade
Join the Bird Rock locals at the Independence Day community event. See dogs, kids, and tricycles decked out in red, white and blue, with crafty kiddie floats, music and goodies.
When: July 4 | Web: birdrock.org
Where: Beaumont Street, Bird Rock (pg. 8).

La Jolla Christmas Parade
See marching bands, beauty queens, floats, equestrians, and an antique aircraft flyover.
When: December, ~first or second weekend.
Web: ljparade.com

OTHER TIDBITS

Best Rummage Sale Ever!
La Jolla United Methodist Church
When: March, 2nd Saturday, 8:30 AM – 2:00 PM.
6063 La Jolla Blvd. | 858.454.7108

The Comedy Store
Stand-up comedians perform nightly.
916 Pearl Street | 858.454.9176

La Jolla Visitor Information Center
7966 Herschel Avenue, #A | 619.236.1212
Winter: Thurs – Tues, 10:00 AM to 5:00 PM.
Summer: Daily 10:00 AM to 7:00 PM.

Local La Jolla Newspapers
La Jolla Light, *La Jolla Village News*
Find free copies at shops and newsstands.

Activities & Shops

La Jolla Shores Sunset

Want Another Copy ?

To purchase a high quality, bound copy of the *La Jolla Guidebook* as a memento or gift, go to **www.LaJollaGuidebook.com** and take advantage of the secure and easy to use, one-click online payment platform. All major credit cards are accepted.

Those with **smart phones** need only scan the QR code below to be taken directly to **www.LaJollaGuidebook.com,** where you can complete the transaction.

To inquire about **advertising opportunities** or to buy books in quantity for **corporate use**, please e-mail derek@LaJollaGuidebook.com or call 858.220.3459.

Locals Guide Publications La Jolla, CA 92037

Ph 858.220.3459 | derek@LaJollaGuidebook.com